ḤADĪTH NOMENCLATURE PRIMERS

نخبة الفكر
Chosen Thoughts

IBN ḤAJAR AL-ʿASQLĀNĪ

التذكرة
The Memorandum

IBN MULAQQIN

ḤADĪTH NOMENCLATURE PRIMERS

نخبة الفكر

IBN ḤAJAR'S

Chosen Thoughts

التذكرة

IBN MULAQQIN'S

The Memorandum

Translation

MUSA FURBER

ḤADĪTH NOMENCLATURE PRIMERS:

1. IBN ḤAJAR AL-ʿASQALĀNĪ'S NUKHBAT AL-FIKAR ("CHOSEN THOUGHTS")

2. IBN MULAQQIN'S AL-TADHKIRAH ("THE MEMORANDUM")

ISBN 978-0-9858840-6-2 (paper)

Published by: Islamosaic (publications@islamosaic.com)

بسم الله الرحمن الرحيم

All praise is to Allah alone, the Lord of the Worlds
And may He send His benedictions upon
our master Muhammad, his Kin
and his Companions
and grant them
peace

TRANSLITERATION KEY

ء	ʾ[1]	ر	r[6]	ف	f
ا	ā, a	ز	z	ق	q[13]
ب	b	س	s	ك	k
ت	t	ش	sh	ل	l
ث	th[2]	ص	ṣ[7]	م	m
ج	j	ض	ḍ[8]	ن	n
ح	ḥ[3]	ط	ṭ[9]	ه	h[14]
خ	kh[4]	ظ	ẓ[10]	و	ū, u, w
د	d	ع	ʿ[11]	ي	ī, i, y
ذ	dh[5]	غ	gh[12]		

1. A distinctive glottal stop made at the bottom of the throat. It is also used to indicate the running of two words into one, e.g., *bismi'Llāh*.
2. Pronounced like the *th* in *think*.
3. Hard *h* sound made at the Adam's apple in the middle of the throat.
4. Pronounced like *ch* in Scottish *loch*.
5. Pronounced like *th* in *this*.
6. A slightly trilled *r* made behind the upper front teeth.
7. An emphatic *s* pronounced behind the upper front teeth.
8. An emphatic *d*-like sound made by pressing the entire tongue against the upper palate.
9. An emphatic *t* sound produced behind the front teeth.
10. An emphatic *th* sound, like the *th* in *this*, make behind the front teeth.
11. A distinctive Semitic sound made in the middle throat and sounding to a Western ear more like a vowel than a consonant.
12. A guttural sound made at the tope of the throat resembling the untrilled German and French *r*.
13. A hard *k* sound produced at the back of the palate.
14. This sound is like the English *h* but has more body. It is made at the very bottom of the throat and pronounced at the beginning, middle, and ends of words.

CONTENTS

المحتويات

TRANSLITERATION KEY VII

TRANSLATOR'S PREFACE VIII

NUKHBAT AL-FIKAR 1

- Introduction 2
- Reports & Their Paths 2
- Uncommonness 4
- Sound Reports 6
- Fair Reports 6
- Additions From Trustworthy Narrators 6
- Contradiction & Objection 8
- The Reject & Its Divisions 8
- Lacunas 10
- Aspersion 12
- To Whom the Report is Attributed 18
- How the Report is Attributed 18
- Forms of Conveyance 22
- Names of Narrators 24
- Conclusion 26
- Miscellaneous Topics 28

AL-TADHKIRAH 33

- Introduction 34
- Categories of Ḥadīths 34
- Types of Report Related Knowledge 36
- Closing 53

INDEX OF TERMS 54

ABOUT THE TRANSLATOR 60

TRANSLATOR'S PREFACE

مقدّمة المترجم

In the Name of Allah, Most Merciful and Compassionate

This book presents two primers on the discipline of ḥadīth nomenclature (*muṣṭalaḥ al-ḥadīth*). The authors kept their primers short to facilitate memorization of the core material and mastery of the discipline. Definitions make up the bulk of these primers, though methods for addressing very specific problems are also included. Students were expected to memorize a short text on the subject. Memorization was not itself the goal. Rather it was a means to facilitate gaining and retaining the more detailed knowledge of the discipline the student would obtain while studying with a living master of the discipline.

This book is intended for the same audience as the original texts: students studying the sciences of ḥadīth and transmission with living instructors. Following their example in concision, I have added only the absolute bare minimum needed to introduce the texts and their authors, and I left explanation for instructors or, if need and opportunity permit, written commentary.

The first primer is *Nukhbat al-fikar* ("Chosen Thoughts on the Nomenclature of Ḥadīth Experts") by Aḥmed bin ʿAlī bin Muḥammad bin Ḥajar al-ʿAsqalānī. Ibn Ḥajar was born in 773AH in Cairo. He died in Cairo in 852AH. (May Allah grant him His Mercy.)

The book has several commentaries, with the best-known being the author's own *Nuzhat al-naẓr*. Both of Ibn Ḥajar's books were well-received by successive generations of scholars and students, and they remain popular to this day.

I translated *Nukhabat al-fikar* sometime between 1999 and 2001. Like most of my short translations, I did it during finals week. During the summer break I translated Ibn Ḥajar's own commentary *Nuzhat al-naẓr*. Although *Nukhbat al-fikar* was well-edited prior to its inclusion in Gibril Fouad Haddad's *Sunnah Notes* (Wardah Publications, 2005), *Nuzhat al-naẓr* is still in line for editing.

The second primer is by one of Ibn Ḥajar's own sheikhs. This second text is *Al-Tadhkirah* ("The Memorandum") by ʿUmar bin ʿAlī bin Aḥmed bin Muḥammad al-Miṣrī al-Shāfiʿī, nicknamed "Ibn al-Mulaqqin." He was born in Cairo 723AH, and died in 804AH. (May Allah grant him His Mercy.)

Ibn Mulaqqin explains that *Al-Tadhkirah* is a summary of his larger work *Al-Muqniʿ*. He wrote a commentary on it named *Al-Tabṣirah*.

I translated *Al-Tadhkirah* in April 2015 after translating his identically named primer on Shāfiʿī law.

It is my hope that these translations serve English-speaking instructors and students as introductions to the basic topics of the subject, and facilitate studying more advanced material. As with the original works, these are intended to be read with a qualified instructor. My recommendation is that Ibn Ḥajar's text should be used as a primary text that is read from beginning to end, sentence by sentence, with an instructor. Instructors can supplement Ibn Ḥajar's text with material unique to Ibn Mulaqqin's text (e.g., items 42–44), and students can read the rest on their own to test their understanding.

The people who helped me with this project are too numerous to mention. I owe a particular debt to Mujīr al-Khaṭīb with whom I had the honor of studying the subject and several of its text. Several friends and fellow students reviewed drafts of the translation and offered innumerable corrections, encouragement, and advice. Shaykh Gibril Haddad deserves specific mention for his role in reviewing and editing *Nukhbat al-fikar* – especially with finding memorable and accurate translations for the nomenclature. Last but not least, I owe much to my wife and children for their constant support and sacrifice throughout the years.

May Allah reward these authors and the people they mentioned therein. May Allah grant all who have been mentioned in this preface (and us!) His mercy, and may He make us among those who benefit from this noble text. Where I have succeeded, it is only through the grace of Allah; where I have faltered it is from my own shortcomings.

Musa Furber
Abu Dhabi
May 5, 2015

نخبة الفكر

Chosen Thoughts on the Nomenclature of Ḥadīth Specialists

by

IBN ḤAJAR AL-ʿASQALĀNĪ

NUKHBAT AL-FIKAR

بسم الله الرحمن الرحيم

1 *Introduction*

Praise to Allah who never ceases being knowing, able. May Allah bless our liegelord Muḥammad, whom He sent to humankind as a bearer of good tidings and a warner, and upon his folk, Companions, and many salutations.

To commence: The books of the nomenclature of ḥadith specialists are many and were expanded and condensed. One of my brothers asked that I summarize for them what is important. I responded to his request seeking to be counted among those who trod the [scholarly] paths. So I say:

2 *Reports & Their Paths*

The paths of a **report** (*khabar*) are either:

1. without specific number
2. more than two paths
3. two paths
4. one path

نخبة الفكر

بسم الله الرحمن الرحيم

١ المقدمة

قال الإمام الحافظ: أحمد ابن علي بن حجر العسقلاني -رحمه الله تعالى-:

الحَمْد لله الَّذي لَمْ يَزَلْ عَالِماً قديراً، وصلَّى اللهُ عَلى سَيِّدِنا مُحَمَّدٍ الَّذي أرْسَلَهُ إلى النَّاس كافَّةً بَشِيراً وَنَذيراً، وعلى آلِ مُحَمَّدٍ وصَحْبِهِ وسَلَّمَ تَسْلِيماً كَثِيراً.

أَمَّا بَعْدُ: فإنَّ التَّصانِيفَ في اصْطلاحِ أهْلِ الحَديثِ قَدْ كَثُرَتْ، وبُسِطَتْ وَاخْتُصِرَتْ، فَسَأَلَنِي بعْضُ الإِخْوَانِ أَنْ أُلَخِّصَ لَهَ المهمَّ مِنْ ذلِكَ، فَأَجَبْتُهُ إلَى سُؤَالِهِ رَجاءَ الانْدِرَاجِ فِي تِلْكَ المَسَالِكِ فأقولُ:

الخَبَرُ إِمَّا أَنْ يَكُونَ لَهُ:

٢ أقسام الخبر باعتبار طرق وصوله إلينا

١- طُرُقٌ بلا عَدَدٍ مُعَيَّنٍ.

٢- أَوْ مَعَ حَصْرٍ بِمَا فَوْقَ الاثْنَيْنِ.

٣- أَوْ بِهِمَا.

٤- أَوْ بِوَاحِدٍ.

- The first is the **mass-transmitted report** (*mutawātir*), and conveys sure knowledge (*'ilm yaqīnī*) when its conditions are met.
- The second is the **well-known report** (*mashhūr*) and it is also called the **well-circulated report** (*mustafīḍ*) according to one opinion.
- The third is the **rare report** (*'azīz*). It is not the [minimal] condition for authenticity, contrary to whoever claimed it.
- The fourth is the **uncommon report** (*gharīb*).

All of them except for the first are **solitary reports** (*āḥād*). They [=these reports] encompass the accepted and the rejected since using them as evidence hinges on investigating the status of the reporters, contrary to the first category. Yet they might contain what conveys inductive knowledge (*'ilm naẓarī*) with external indicators, according to the preferred opinion.

3 *Uncommonness*

Then the **uncommonness** (*gharāba*) is either:

1. at the root of the **chain** (*sanad*)
2. or not.

- The first is the **absolutely-unique report** (*fard muṭlaq*) [e.g. one-ḥadīth narrator, one-compiler narrator, one-narrator ḥadīth, one-locality narrations].
- The second is the **relatively-unique report** (*fard nisbī*), and it is rare that the term '**unique**' (*fard*) is used for it without qualification.

فالأَوَّلُ: المُتَوَاتِرُ المُفيدُ لِلْعِلْمِ الْيَقِينيّ بِشُرُوطِهِ.
والثَّانِي: المَشْهُورُ وَهُوَ المُسْتَفِيضُ عَلَى رَأْيٍ.
والثَّالِثُ: الْعَزِيزُ، وَلَيْسَ شَرْطًا لِلصَّحِيحِ، خِلافاً لِمَنْ زَعَمَهُ.
والرَّابعُ: الغَرِيبُ.
وَكُلُّها -سِوَى الأَوَّلِ- آحَادٌ، وفيها المَقْبُولُ والمَرْدُودُ، لِتَوَقُّفِ الاسْتِدْلالِ بها عَلى البَحْث عنْ أَحْوالِ رُوَاتِها، دُونَ الأَوَّل، وَقَدْ يَقَع فيها مَا يُفيدُ العِلمَ النَّظَرِيَّ بالقرائنِ على المُخْتَار.

٣ الغرابة

ثمَّ الغَرابَةُ: إمَّا أَنْ تكُونَ
١. فِي أَصْلِ السَّنَدِ،
٢. أَوْ لا.
فالأَوَّلُ: الفَرْدُ المُطْلَقُ.
والثاني: الْفَرْدُ النّسْبِيُّ، ويَقِلُّ إطْلاقُ الفَرْدِيّةِ عليهِ.

4 *Sound Reports*

The **solitary report** (*āḥād*) transmitted by:

1. an **upright** (*'adl*)
2. **thoroughly accurate** person (*tāmm al-ḍabṭ*)
3. with a **continuous chain** (*sanad*)
4. that is not **defective** (*mu'allal*)
5. nor **anomalous** (*shādhdh*)

is the **sound-in-itself report** (*ṣaḥīḥ bi-dhātihi*). Its ranks are commensurate to variation in these conditions. Hence al-Bukhārī's Ṣaḥīḥ was put first, then Muslim's, and then what matches their criteria (*shurūṭ*).

5 *Fair Reports*

If the accuracy decreases then it is the **fair-in-itself report** (*ḥasan li-dhātihi*); with multiple paths it is considered **sound** (*ṣaḥīḥ*).

If the grading is composite [e.g. **fair-sound** (*ḥasan ṣaḥīḥ*)] it is [either] because of indecision regarding the reporter when it [=his report] is unique [either fair or sound]; otherwise it is from examining two chains [one fair and one sound].

6 *Additions from Trustworthy Narrators*

An addition from a narrator of each of these two types of chains [the sound and the fair] is accepted as long as his addition does not negate [the report of] someone who is more trustworthy.

- If the addition is contrary to something superior (*arjaḥ*), the stronger is the **well-preserved report** (*maḥfūẓ*), and its opposite is the **anomalous report** (*shādhdh*).

٤ الصحيح لذاته

وَخَبَرُ الآحَادِ بِنَقْلِ

١. عَدْلٍ

٢. تَامِّ الضَّبْطِ،

٣. متَّصِلَ السَّنَدِ،

٤. غيرَ مُعَلَّلٍ

٥. وَلا شَاذٍّ

هُوَ الصَّحِيحُ لِذَاتِه. وتَتَفَاوتُ رُتبُهُ بِتفَاوُتِ هذِهِ الأوْصَافِ. وَمِنْ ثمَّ قُدِّمَ صَحِيحُ البُخَارِيّ، ثُمَّ مُسْلمٍ، ثُمَّ شَرْطُهُمَا.

٥ الحسن لذاته

فإنَّ خَفَّ الضَّبْطُ: فالحَسَنُ لِذَاتِهِ، وبِكَثْرَةِ طُرُقِهِ يُصَحَّحُ.

فإنْ جُمِعَا فلِلتَّرَدُّدِ في النّاقِلِ حَيْثُ التَّفَرُّدُ، وإلا فباعْتِبَارِ إسْنادَيْنِ.

٦ زيادة الثقة وأقسامها

وزِيَادَةُ رَاوِيهِمَا مَقْبُولَةٌ ما لَمْ تَقعْ مُنَافِيَةً لِمَنْ هُوَ أَوْثَقُ.

فإِنْ خُولِفَ بِأَرْجَحَ فَالرَّاجِحُ الْمَحْفُوظُ، وَمُقَابِلُهُ الشَّاذُّ،

- If in addition to being contrary it is **weak** (*ḍaʿīf*), the stronger is the **well-recognized** (*maʿrūf*), and its opposite is the **disclaimed report** (*munkar*).

When a report agrees with a **relatively-unique report** (*fard nisbī*) it is called a **corroborative chain** (*mutābiʿ*).

If a report's content (*matn*) is found that resembles it, then it is a **witness-report** (*shāhid*).

Investigating the paths of transmission for the above is called **evaluation** (*iʿtibār*).

7 *Contradiction & Objection*

That which is **accepted** (*maqbūl*):

- If it is free from **contradiction or objection** (*muʿāraḍa*), then it is **decisive** (*muḥkam*).
- If it is contradicted by something equal to it [in soundness]:
    - if **reconciliation** (*jamʿ*) is possible, they are **reconcilable reports** (*mukhtalif al-ḥadīth*);
    - if not and the later one is **positively established** (*thābit*), then one is the **abrogating report** (*nāsikh*) and the other is the **abrogated report** (*mansūkh*);
    - if not, **superiority is sought** (*tarjīḥ*);
    - and lastly, neither one is confirmed or denied (*tawaqquf*)

8 *The Rejected & its Divisions*

Reports are rejected because of:

1. **lacuna** (*saqṭ*)
2. or **aspersion** (*ṭaʿn*).

وَمَعَ الضَّعْفِ فالرَّاجِحُ المَعْرُوفُ، وَمُقَابِلُهُ المُنْكَرُ.
وَالْفَرْدُ النِّسْبِيّ: إنْ وَافَقَه غيره فَهُوَ المُتَابِعُ.
وَإِنْ وُجِدَ مَتْنٌ يَشْبَهُهُ فَهُوَ الشَّاهِدُ.
وتَتَبُّعُ الطّرُقِ لذلك هو الاعتبار.

٧ المعارضة والاخالاف

ثم المقبول:
إِنْ سَلِمَ مِنَ المعارضة فهو المُحْكَمَ،
وإنْ عُورض بِمثْلِهِ:
فإنْ أمْكَنَ الجَمْعُ فمُخْتَلِفُ الحَدِيث،
أو لا، وثَبَتَ المُتَأَخِّرُ فهُوَ النَّاسِخُ، والآخَرُ المَنْسُوخُ،
وإلاَّ فَالتّرْجِيحُ،
ثمَّ التَّوَقُّفُ.

٨ المردود وأقسامه

ثم المردود: إمّا أن يكونَ
١. لِسقْطٍ
٢. أو طَعْنٍ.

9 *Lacunas*

Lacunas are either:

1. at the beginning of the **chain** (*sanad*) on the part of the compiler,
2. at the end of the chain after the Successor (may Allah be pleased with them),
3. or elsewhere.

- The first [case] is the **suspended report** (*mu'allaq*).
- The second is the **expedient report** (*mursal*).
- The third:
    - If the lacuna consists in two or more narrators consecutively then it is the **problematic report** (*mu'ḍal*),
    - If not, then it is the **broken-chained report** (*munqaṭi'*).

The lacunas can be:

1. obvious,
2. or hidden.

- The first is recognized by lack of meeting [between inter-connected reporters]. Hence the need for [biographical] history.
- The second is the **camouflaged report** (*mudallas*), a report related with a phrase which implies possible meeting, such as "From so-and-so", "He said...", (*'an*, *qāla*). Likewise, the **hidden expedient report** (*mursal khafī*) from a contemporary he did not meet [or did not meet as a narrator, such as a baby Companion from the Prophet ﷺ, e.g. Mūsā ibn Ṭalḥa (May Allah be pleased with him)].

٩ المردود للسقط

فالسَّقْطُ: إمَّا أنْ يكونَ

١. مِنْ مَبَادِيءِ السَّنَدِ مِنْ مُصَنِّفٍ،

٢. أَوْ مِنْ آخِرِهِ بَعدَ التَّابِعيّ،

٣. أَوْ غيْرِ ذَلِكَ.

فالأَوَّلُ: المُعَلَّقُ.

والثَّانِي: المُرْسَلُ.

والثَّالِثُ: إنْ كانَ باثْنَيْن فَصَاعِداً مَعَ التَّوَالي، فُهو المُعْضَلُ، وَإلاَّ فالمُنْقَطِعُ.

ثُمَّ قَدْ يَكُونُ

١. واضِحاً

٢. أَوْ خَفِيّاً.

فالأَوَّلُ: يُدْرَكُ بعَدَمِ التَّلاقي، وَمِنْ ثمَّ احْتِيجَ إِلَى التَّأريخِ.

وَالثَّانِي: المُدَلَّسُ، وَيَرِدُ بِصِيغَةٍ تَحْتَمِلُ اللُّقِيَّ: كَعَنْ، وَقَالَ، وَكَذَا المُرْسَلُ الخَفِيُّ مِنْ مُعَاصِرٍ لمْ يَلْقَ.

10 *Aspersion*

Aspersion (*ṭaʿn*) is because of one of the following:

1. the narrator lying
2. being accused of lying
3. making enormous mistakes
4. being heedless (*ghaflah*)
5. being morally corrupt (*fāsiq*)
6. being delusionary (*wahm*)
7. contradicting others (*mukhālafah*)
8. being unknown (*jahālah*)
9. being an innovator
10. being chronically forgetful

- The first is the **forged report** (*mawḍūʿ*).
- The second is the **discarded report** (*matrūk*).
- The third is the **disclaimed report** (*munkar*) according to one opinion, as are the fourth and fifth.
- When **delusion** (*wahm*) is discovered through **external indications** (*qarāʾin*) and gathering the paths of transmission, then it is the defective report (*muʿallal*).
- As for **contradicting others** (*mukhālafa*), if it results from:
  - changing the wording of the chain, it is the **chain-interpolated report** *(mudraj al-isnād*)
  - conflating a **halted Companion-report** (*mawqūf*) with a raised Prophetic-report (*marfūʿ*) then it is the **content-interpolated report** (*mudraj al-matn*)
  - or transposition, then the **topsy-turvy report** (*maqlūb*)
  - or inserting a narrator, then it is the insertion into an **already-connected-chain report** (*mazīd fī muttaṣil al-masānīd*)

١٠ الطعن في الراوي وأسبابه]

ثم الطعن: إمَّا أنْ يَكُونَ:

١. لِكَذِبِ الرَّاوِي.

٢. أَوْ تُهْمَتِهِ بِذلِكَ.

٣. أَوْ فُحْشِ غَلَطِهِ.

٤. أَوْ غَفْلَتِهِ.

٥. أَوْ فِسْقِهِ.

٦. أَوْ وَهْمِهِ.

٧. أَوْ مُخَالَفَتِه.

٨. أَوْ جَهَالَتِه.

٩. أَوْ بِدْعَتِهِ.

١٠. أو سُوءِ حِفْظِهِ.

فالأَوَّلُ: المَوْضُوعُ،
والثَّانِي: المَتْرُوكُ.
والثَّالِثُ: المُنْكَرُ، عَلَى رَأْيٍ. وكَذَا الرَّابِعُ والخَامِسُ.
ثمَّ الوَهْمُ: إِنِ اطُّلِعَ عَلَيْهِ بِالقَرَائِنِ وَجَمْعِ الطُّرُقِ: فَالمُعَلَّلُ.

ثمَّ المُخَالَفَةُ: إنْ كانَتْ
بِتَغْيِيرِ السِّيَاقِ: فَمُدْرَجُ الإِسْنَادِ.
أَوْ بِدَمْجِ مَوْقوفٍ بِمرْفوعٍ: فَمُدْرَجُ المَتْنِ.
أَوْ بِتَقْدِيمٍ أَوْ تَأْخِيرٍ: فَالمَقْلُوبُ.
أَوْ بِزِيَادَةِ رَاوٍ: فَالمَزِيدُ في مُتَّصِلِ الأسانيدِ.

- or it is substituting one narrator for another [without preponderance of one chain over the other], then it is the **inconsistent report** (*muḍṭarib*). Substitution may occur intentionally for the sake of testing
- or alternating dots or vowels while orthography remains the same, then the **dot-distorted report** (*muṣaḥḥaf*) and the **vowel-distorted report** (*muḥarraf*).
- It is not permissible to intentionally alter a ḥadīth's **content** (*matn*) by omission or paraphrase, except for someone knowledgeable of what changes meanings.
- If the meaning is obscure, explaining odd words and clarifying the problematic is needed.

- The causes for which a **narrator is unknown** (*jahāla*) are:
  - The narrator may have many names and he is mentioned with one that is not well-known, for a purpose. Concerning this they compiled the **clarifier** (*al-mūḍiḥ*).
  - The narrator has few [narrations] and is not frequently taken from. Concerning this they wrote **single-report narrators** (*al-wuḥdān*).
  - Or he may be left unnamed out of brevity. Concerning this [they compiled] the **anonymous mentions** (*mubhamāt*).
  - The **anonymous narrator** (*mubham*) is not accepted, even if he is mentioned anonymously with a grading of **commendation** (*ta'dīl*), according to the soundest opinion.
  - If the narrator is named:
    - If only one person related from him, then he is an **unidentifiable reporter** (*majhūl al-'ayn*).
    - If two or more related from him and he is not [explicitly] declared reliable, then he is a **reporter of unknown status** (*majhūl al-ḥāl*); and that is the **veiled reporter** (*mastūr*).

أَوْ بِإِبْدَالِهِ وَلَا مُرَجِّحَ: فَالْمُضطَرِبُ -وَقَدْ يَقَعُ الإِبْدَالُ عَمْداً امْتِحَاناً.

أَوْ بِتَغْيِيرِ حَرْفٍ، أَوْ حُرُوفٍ مَعَ بَقَاءِ السِّيَاقِ: فَالْمُصَحَّفُ وَالْمُحَرَّفُ.

وَلَا يَجُوزُ تَعَمُّدُ تَغْيِيرِ الْمَتْنِ بِالنَّقْصِ وَالْمُرَادِفِ إِلَّا لِعَالِمٍ بِمَا يُحِيلُ الْمَعَانِي.

فَإِنْ خَفِيَ الْمَعْنَى احْتِيجَ إِلَى شَرْحِ الْغَرِيبِ وَبَيَانِ الْمُشْكِلِ.

ثُمَّ الْجَهَالَةُ: وَسَبَبُهَا أَنَّ:

الرَّاوِيَ قَدْ تَكْثُرُ نُعُوتُهُ فَيُذْكَرُ بِغَيْرِ مَا اشْتَهَرَ بِهِ لِغَرَضٍ، وَصَنَّفُوا فِيهِ الْمُوضِحَ.

وَقَدْ يَكُونُ مُقِلّاً فَلَا يَكْثُرُ الأَخْذُ عَنْهُ، وَصَنَّفُوا فِيهِ الْوُحْدَانَ.

أَوْ لَا يُسَمَّى اخْتِصَاراً، وَفِيهِ الْمُبْهَمَاتُ.

وَلَا يُقْبَلُ الْمُبْهَمُ، وَلَوْ أُبْهِمَ بِلَفْظِ التَّعْدِيلِ، عَلَى الأَصَحِّ.

فَإِنْ سُمِّيَ:

وَانْفَرَدَ وَاحِدٌ عَنْهُ فَمَجْهُولُ الْعَيْنِ،

أَوِ اثْنَانِ فَصَاعِداً وَلَمْ يُوَثَّقْ: فَمَجْهُولُ الحَالِ، وَهُوَ الْمَسْتُورُ.

- Innovation is of two types:
  1. tantamount to apostasy
  2. or tantamount to moral corruption.

  As for the first: The vast majority do not accept any narrator thus described.

  As for the second: Someone who is not inviting people to it is accepted according to the soundest opinion, unless he related something supporting his innovation: in that case he is rejected according to the preferred opinion. This is what al-Nasā'ī's shaykh, al-Jūzajānī, explicitly said.

- Then poor memory:
  - If it is chronic, then it is the **anomalous report** (*shādhdh*) according to one opinion
  - or occasional, then the **jumbled report** (*mukhtalaṭ*).
  - Whenever a chronically-forgetful reporter is corroborated by a reporter worthy of consideration, the **veiled reporter** (*mastūr*), the **expedient reporter** (*mursil*), and likewise the camouflager-reporter (*mudallis*), their ḥadīth becomes the **fair** (*ḥasan*) report, **not in itself, but on the whole** (*lā li-dhātihi bal bil-majmū'*).

ثمَّ البِدْعَةُ: إمَّا

١. بمُكَفِّرٍ،

٢. أو بِمُفَسِّقٍ.

فالأوَّلُ: لا يَقْبَلُ صَاحِبَها الجمهورُ.

والثّاني: يُقبَلُ مَنْ لَم يكُنْ دَاعِيةً، في الأصَحّ، إلاَّ إِنْ رَوَى مَا يُقوِّي بدْعَتَهُ فيُرَدُّ، عَلَى المُخْتَارِ، وَبِهِ صَرَّحَ الجوزجانيُّ شَيْخُ النَّسائِي.

ثمَّ سُوءُ الحِفْظِ: إنْ كانَ لازماً فهُوَ الشَّاذُّ عَلَى رَأْيٍ، أَوْ طارِئاً فالمُخْتَلِطُ.

وَمَتَى تُوبِعَ سَيِّءُ الحِفْظِ بِمُعْتَبَرٍ، وَكَذَا المَسْتُورُ، وَالمُرْسَلُ، وَالمُدَلَّسُ: صَارَ حَدِيثُهُمْ حَسَناً لا لِذَاتِهِ، بَلْ بالمَجْمُوعِ.

11 *To Whom the Report is Attributed*

The chain's **ascription** (*isnād*) explicitly or implicitly goes to

1. the Prophet ﷺ: consisting in his statements, or his actions, or his tacit approval
2. a Companion (May Allah be pleased with him). He is whoever encountered the Prophet ﷺ believing in him and died as a Muslim, even if [his Islam] was interrupted by apostasy according to the strongest opinion
3. or a Successor, namely anyone who met one of the Companions.

- The first is the **raised-chain (Prophetic) report** (*marfū'*).
- The second is the **halted-chain (Companion) report** (*mawqūf*).
- The third is the **severed-chain (sub-Companion) report** (*maqṭū'*). It is the same for anyone subsequent to the Successor.
- The last two are said to be **non-Prophetic reports** (*āthār*).

12 *How the Report is Attributed*

A **grounded report** (*musnad*) is a report that a Companion raised to the Prophet ﷺ with a chain that has the outward appearance of being connected. If its numbers [of narrators in the chain] are few, either it ends with:

1. the Prophet ﷺ
2. or an Imām with a distinguished description, like Shu'ba.

- The first is **absolute elevation** (*'ulūw muṭlaq*)
- The second is **relative elevation** (*'ulūw nisbī*). It includes:
  - **concurrent chain** (*muwāfaqa*) which arrives at the shaykh of one of the compilers without using the compiler's path;

١١ الإسناد

ثم الإسناد: إمَّا أَنْ يَنْتَهِيَ إِلَى النَّبِي صلَّى اللهُ عليه وسلم تَصْرِيحاً، أَوْ حُكْماً: مِنْ قَوْلِه، أَوْ فِعْلِهِ، أَوْ تقْرِيره.

أَوْ إِلَى الصَّحَابِيِّ كَذلِك: وَهُوَ: مَنْ لَقِي النَّبِيَّ صلى الله عليه وسلم، مُؤمِناً بِهِ وَمَاتَ عَلَى الإِسْلام: وَلَوْ تَخَلَّلَتْ رِدَّةٌ، في الأَصَحِّ.

أَوْ إِلى التَّابِعِيِّ: وَهُوَ مَنْ لَقِيَ الصَّحَابِيَّ كَذلِكَ.

فَالأَوَّل: المَرفوعُ،

والثَّانِي: المَوْقُوفُ،

والثَّالِثُ: المَقْطوعُ، وَمَنْ دونَ التَّابِعِيّ فيه مِثْلُهُ.

وَيُقَالُ للأخِيرَيْنِ: الأَثَرُ.

والمسنَدُ: مرفوع صحَابيٍّ بسَنَدٍ ظَاهِره الاتّصال. فإن قَلَّ عَدَدُهُ: فإمَّا أَنْ يَنْتَهِي

١. إلى النَّبيّ صلَّى اللهُ عليه وسلم،

٢. أَوْ إلى إِمَام ذِي صِفَةٍ عَلِيَّةٍ كشُعْبَة.

فالأَوَّلُ: العُلُوُّ المُطْلَق.

والثَّاني: النِّسْبِيُّ.

وَفِيهِ المُوافقَةُ: وَهِيَ الْوُصُولُ إلى شَيْخِ أَحَدِ المُصنِّفِينَ مِنْ غَيْرِ طَرِيقِهِ.

وفِيهِ الْبَدَلُ: وَهُوَ الْوُصُولُ إِلى شَيْخِ شَيْخِهِ كَذلِك.

- **convergent chain** (*badal*) which arrives at the shaykh's shaykh in the same way;
- **parity** (*musāwāt*) which is the number of narrator-links in the chain from the narrator to the end equaling [the length of] the chains of one of the compilers;
- and **handshaking** (*muṣāfaḥah*) which equals the chain of that compiler's student.

Descent (*nuzūl*) corresponds to **elevation** (*'ulūw*) in all of its categories.

If the narrator is the same age as someone who narrates from him and they met, then it is **peer narration** (*aqrān*).

If each of them related from each other then it is **reciprocal narration** (*mudabbaj*).

If he relates from someone inferior [in age, teachers or knowledge] him, then it is **seniors-from-juniors narration** (*akābir 'an aṣāghir*). It includes: **fathers-from-sons narration** (*al-ābā' 'an al-abnā'*); its opposite is frequent. It includes **son-from-father or grandfather narration** (*'an abīhi 'an jaddihi*).

If two share the same shaykh and one's death precedes, then it is **predecessor-successor narration** (*sābiq wa-lāḥiq*).

If he relates from two shaykhs whose names match and cannot be differentiated, then the fact that he specializes in narrations from one of them is a sign that the other one is irrelevant.

If he denies what is related from him

- categorically, the report is rejected
- or possibly, then it is accepted according to the soundest opinion.

وَفيهِ المُسَاوَاةُ: وَهِيَ اسْتِوَاءُ عَدَدِ الإِسْنَادِ مِنَ الرَّاوِي إلى آخِرِهِ مَعَ إِسْنَادِ أَحَدِ المُصَنِّفِينَ.

وفيهِ المُصَافَحَةُ: وهِيَ الاسْتِوَاءُ مَعَ تِلْمِيذِ ذَلِكَ المُصَنِّفِ.

وَيُقَابِلُ الْعُلُوَّ بِأَقْسَامِهِ النُّزُولُ،

فإِنْ تَشَارَكَ الرَّاوِي وَمَنْ رَوَى عَنْهُ في السِّنِّ واللُّقِيِّ فهو الأَقْرَانُ.

وَإِنْ رَوَى كُلٌّ مِنْهُمَا عنِ الآخَرِ: فَالمُدَبَّجُ.

وَإِنْ رَوَى عَمَّنْ دُونَه: فالأكابِرُ عن الأَصَاغِرِ، وَمِنْه الآباءُ عَن الأَبْنَاء، وفي عَكْسِهِ كثْرَةٌ، وَمِنْهُ مَنْ رَوَى عَنْ أَبِيهِ عَنْ جَدِّهِ.

وإِنِ اشْتَرَكَ اثنَانِ عَنْ شَيْخٍ، وَتَقَدَّمَ مَوْتُ أَحَدِهِما، فَهُوَ: السَّابِقُ واللاَّحِقُ.

وإِنْ رَوَى عَن اثنَيْنِ مُتَّفِقي الاسْمِ وَلَمْ يَتَمَيَّزَا، فباخْتِصَاصِه بِأَحدِهِمَا يَتَبَيَّنُ المُهْمَلُ.

وإن جَحَدَ مَرْوِيَّهُ

١. جَزْماً: رُدَّ،

٢. أَوِ احْتِمالاً: قُبِلَ، في الأصحِّ.

Concerning this is the genre of **those-who-narrated-and-forgot** (*man ḥaddatha wa-nasiya*).

If the narrators conform in the phrasing used to convey or in some other manner, then it is pattern-chained narration (*musalsal*).

13 *Forms of Conveyance*

The forms of conveyance are:

1. "*Samiʿtu*" (I heard)
2. and "*ḥaddathanī*" (he narrated to me)
3. then "*akhbaranī*" (he reported to me)
4. and "*qara'tu ʿalayhi*" (I read to him)
5. then "*quri'a ʿalayhi wa-ana asmaʿu*" (it was read to him while I heard)
6. then "*anba'anī*" (he informed me)
7. then "*nāwalanī*" (he put into my hands)
8. then "*shāfahanī*" (he told me verbally)
9. then "*kataba ilayya*" (he wrote to me)
10. then "from" ("*ʿan*") and the like.

- The first two are for someone who heard the shaykh verbatim one-on-one. If pluralized then [he heard] with someone else. The first is the most explicit and is the highest-ranked in ḥadīth dictation.
- The third and forth are for someone who read [to the shaykh] while alone. If the plural is used it is like the fifth.
- Informing [the sixth] is synonymous with reporting [the third]. However, in the custom of the later generations it is for **authorization** (*ijāzah*), like an *ʿan* [from].

وفيه: «مَنْ حَدَّث وَنَسِيَ».
وإن اتفقَ الرُّواةُ في صِيَعِ الأداءِ، أَوْ غَيْرِهَا مِنَ الحَالاتِ، فَهُو المُسَلْسَلُ.

١٢ صيغ الأداء ومراتبها

وصيغ الأداء:
١- سُمِعْتُ.
٢- وَحَدَّثَنِي.
٣- ثمَّ أَخْبَرَنِي،
٤- وَقَرَأْتُ عَلَيْه.
٥- ثمَّ قُرِئَ عَلَيْهِ وَأَنا أَسْمَعُ.
٦- ثمَّ أَنْبَأَنِي.
٧- ثمَّ نَاوَلَنِي.
٨- ثمَّ شَافَهَنِي.
٩- ثمَّ كَتَبَ إِلَيَّ.
١٠- ثمَّ عَنْ، وَنَحْوُهَا.
فَالأَوَّلانِ: لِمَنْ سَمِعَ وَحْدَهُ مِنْ لَفْظِ الشَّيْخِ، فَإِنْ جَمَعَ فمعَ غَيْرِهِ.
وأَوَّلُهَا: أصرحُها وَأَرْفعُها فِي الإِمْلاءِ.
والثَّالِثُ، والرَّابعُ: لِمَنْ قَرَأَ بِنَفْسِهِ، فإِنْ جَمَعَ: فَكَالْخَامِسِ.
والإِنْبَاءُ: بمَعْنَى الإِخْبَارِ، إِلاَّ في عُرْفِ المُتَأَخِّرينَ فَهُوَ للإِجازَةِ كَعَنْ.

- The **indecisive-transmission terminology** [*ʿanʿana*, i.e. "from so-and-so, from so-and-so"] of contemporaries is understood to be direct audition unless from a **camouflaging reporter** (*mudallis*). It is said that a condition is that the meeting of the said contemporaries be positively proven, even if only once; it is the preferred opinion (*mukhtār*).
- They used *mushāfahah* for an oral authorization and *mukātaba* for a written authorization [with the late scholars].
- For the authenticity of *munāwala*, they stipulated that it be accompanied by permission to relate; it is the highest type of authorization (*ijāzah*).
- They also stipulated permission for a report **found** (*wijāda*, i.e. "something found in a book"), likewise a book **bequeathed** (*waṣiyya bil-kitāb*), and in a shaykh's **public announcement** that he narrates something (*iʿlām*), otherwise it is of no consequence; as is an authorization that is universal or to someone unknown [to us], or to someone nonexistent—according to the soundest opinion concerning all of the above.

14 *Names of Narrators*

If the names of the narrators and the names of their fathers and on up match although they are different individuals, then it is **same-name different-identity narrator** (*muttafiq wa-muftariq*).

If the names match in writing but differ in pronunciation, then it is **homographic-heterophonic** (*mu'talif wa-mukhtalif*).

If the names match but differ in their fathers, or the opposite, it is **same-name different-father-or-son narrators** (*mutashābih*), and likewise if the similarity occurred in the name and the name of the father while there is a difference in the **affiliation** (*nisbah*).

وَعَنْعَنَةُ الْمُعَاصِرِ مَحْمُولَةٌ عَلَى السَّمَاعِ إلاَّ مِنَ المُدَلِّسِ. وَقِيلَ: يُشْتَرَطُ ثُبُوتُ لِقَائِهِمَا وَلَوْ مَرَّةً، وهُوَ المُخْتَارُ.

وَأَطْلَقُوا المُشَافَهَةَ فِي الإِجَازَةِ المُتَلَفَّظِ بِهَا، وَالمُكَاتَبَةَ فِي الإِجَازَةِ المُكْتُوبِ بِهَا.

واشْتَرَطُوا فِي صِحَّةِ المُنَاوَلَةِ اقْتِرَانَهَا بِالإِذْنِ بِالرِّوَايَةِ، وَهِيَ أَرْفَعُ أَنْوَاعِ الإِجَازَةِ.

وَكَذَا اشْتَرَطُوا الإِذْنَ فِي الوِجَادَةِ، وَالْوَصِيَّةِ بِالْكِتَابِ، وَفِي الإِعْلَامِ، وَإلاَّ فَلاَ عِبْرَةَ بِذلِكَ، كالإِجَازَةِ الْعَامَّةِ، وَلِلْمَجْهُولِ، وَلِلْمَعْدُومِ، عَلَى الأَصَحِّ فِي جَمِيعِ ذلِكَ.

١٣ الرواة

ثمَّ الرُّوَاةُ: إِنِ اتَّفَقَتْ أَسْمَاؤُهُمْ وَأَسْمَاءُ آبَائِهِمْ فَصَاعِداً، واخْتَلَفَتْ أَشْخَاصُهُمْ: فَهُوَ المُتَّفِقُ وَالمُفْتَرَقُ،

وإِنِ اتَّفَقَتِ الأَسْمَاءُ خَطّاً واخْتَلَفَتْ نُطْقاً: فَهُوَ المُؤْتَلِفُ وَالمُخْتَلِفُ.

وإِنِ اتَّفَقَتِ الأَسْمَاءُ واخْتَلَفَتِ الآبَاءُ، أَوْ بِالعكْسِ: فَهُوَ المُتَشَابِهُ، وَكَذَا إنْ وَقَعَ الاتِّفَاقُ فِي الاسْمِ واسْمِ الأَبِ، والاخْتِلاَفُ فِي النِّسْبَةِ،

This and the previous can form various combinations, including:

- similarity or difference occurring except in one or two letters
- or transposition
- or the like.

15 Conclusion

It is also important to know:

1. the synchronous layers (*ṭabaqāt*) of narrators
2. the dates of their birth and death
3. their lands and regions
4. and their conditions: **commendation** (*taʿdīl*), **discreditation** (*jarḥ*), and **being unknown** (*jahālah*).

The **categories of discreditation** (*jarḥ*) are [from worst to slight]:

1. To be described with the superlative (*afʿal*), e.g. "greatest of all liars" ("*akdhab al-nās*")
2. "Arch-imposter", "arch-fabricator", "arch-liar" ("*dajjāl*", "*waḍḍāʿ*", or "*kadhdhāb*")
3. The slightest is "malleable", "chronically forgetful", and "he leaves something to be desired" ("*layyin*", "*sayyiʾ al-ḥifẓ*", and "*fīhi maqāl*").

And the **ranks of commendation** (*taʿdīl*) are [from highest to lowest]:

1. To be described with the superlative (afʿal), e.g. "most trustworthy of people" ("*awthaq al-nās*")
2. What is emphasized with one attribute or two, e.g. "trustworthy-trustworthy", "trustworthy and memorizer" ("*thiqah thiqah*" or "*thiqah ḥāfiẓ*")
3. Something that suggests proximity to the slightest levels of discreditation, e.g. "honest layman" ("*shaykh*").

وَيَتَرَكَّبُ مِنْهُ وَمِمَّا قَبْلَهُ أَنْوَاعٌ:

مِنْها أَنْ يَحْصُلَ الاتِّفَاقُ أَوِ الاشْتِبَاهُ إِلاَّ في حَرْفٍ أَوْ حَرْفَيْنِ.

أَوْ بِالتَّقْدِيمِ وَالتَّأْخِيرِ.

أَوْ نَحْوِ ذَلِكَ.

١٤ خاتمة

وَمِنَ الْمُهِمِّ: مَعْرِفَةُ

١. طَبَقَاتِ الرُّوَاةِ

٢. وَمَوَالِيدِهِمْ، وَوَفَيَاتِهِمْ،

٣. وَبُلْدَانِهِمْ،

٤. وَأَحْوَالِهِمْ: تَعْدِيلاً وَتَجْرِيحاً وَجَهَالَةً.

وَمَرَاتِبُ الْجَرْحِ:

١. وَأَسْوَأُهَا الْوَصْفُ بِأَفْعَلَ، كَأَكْذَبِ النَّاسِ،

٢. ثُمَّ دَجَّالٌ، أَوْ وَضَّاعٌ، أَوْ كَذَّابٌ.

٣. وَأَسْهَلُهَا: لَيِّنٌ، أَوْ سَيِّئُ الْحِفْظِ، أَوْ فيه مَقَالٌ.

ومراتب التعديل:

١. وَأرفعها الْوَصْفُ بِأَفْعَلَ: كَأَوْثَقِ النَّاسِ،

٢. ثُمَّ مَا تَأَكَّدَ بِصِفَةٍ أَوْ صِفَتَيْنِ، كِثِقَةٌ ثِقَةٌ، أَوْ ثِقَةٌ حافظٌ.

٣. وَأَدْنَاهَا مَا أَشْعَرَ بِالقُرْبِ مِنْ أَسْهَلِ التَّجْرِيحِ، كَـ: شَيْخٌ.

Attesting someone's good record (*tazkiya*) is accepted from someone knowledgeable in its criteria, even if from a single person according to the soundest opinion (*aṣaḥḥ*).

Discreditation (*jarḥ*) takes precedence over commendation (*taʿdīl*) if it comes in detail from someone knowledgeable in its criteria. When lacking commendation, discreditation is accepted without specifics, according to the preferred opinion (*mukhtār*).

16 Miscellaneous Topics

It is also important to know:

- **agnomens** (*kunā*, sing. *kunya*) of the people referred to by [first] name,
- the names of people referred to by agnomen,
- those whose agnomen and name are one and the same,
- those with multiple agnomens or multiple titles;
- the one whose agnomen matches his father's name,
- or vice-versa;
- or his agnomen [matches] his wife's agnomen;
- and whoever is affiliated to someone other than his father or is affiliated to his mother,
- or to something that does not immediately come to mind;
- and whose name matches the name of his father and his grandfather,
- or his shaykh's name and the shaykh's shaykh, and on up;
- and whose name matches the shaykh's name and the person narrating from him;
- and the basic names of narrators;

وَتُقْبَلُ التَّزْكِيَةُ مِنْ عَارِفٍ بِأَسْبَابِها، ولو مِن واحدٍ، على الأَصَحِّ.

والجَرْحُ مُقَدَّمٌ عَلَى التَّعْدِيلِ إِنْ صَدَرَ مُبَيَّناً مِن عَارِفٍ بِأَسْبَابِه، فَإِنْ خَلاَ عَن التَّعْدِيلِ: قُبِلَ مُجْمَلاً، عَلَى المُخْتَارِ.

١٥ فصل معرفة الكنى وغيرها

وَمِنَ المُهِمِّ مَعْرِفَةُ

كُنَى المُسَمَّيْنَ،

وأَسْمَاءِ المُكَنَّيْنَ،

وَمَن اسْمُهُ كُنْيَتُهُ،

ومِنِ اخْتُلِفَ في كُنْيَتِه،

ومن كَثُرَتْ كُنَاهُ أو نُعُوتُهُ،

وَمَنْ وَافَقَتْ كُنْيَتُهُ اسْمَ أَبِيهِ،

أَوْ بِالعَكْسِ،

أَوْ كُنْيَتُهُ كُنْيَةَ زَوْجَتِهِ،

وَمَنْ نُسِبَ إِلَى غَيْرِ أَبِيهِ، أَوْ إِلى أُمِّهِ،

أَوْ إِلى غير ما يَسْبِقُ إلى الفَهْمِ،

ومن اتَّفَقَ اسْمُهُ واسْمُ أَبِيهِ وجَدِّهِ،

أو اسْمُ شَيْخِهِ وشَيْخِ شَيْخِهِ فَصَاعِداً.

وَمَن اتَّفَقَ اسْمُ شَيْخِهِ والرَّاوي عنهُ.

وَمَعْرِفَةُ الأَسْمَاءِ المُجَرَّدِةِ

- and the **names exclusive to one person** (*mufrada*),
- and agnomens and nicknames.

[It is also important to know:)

- Affiliations, i.e. to tribes, homelands, countries, localities, roads and alleys, proximity; to crafts and professions. It gives rise to **similarities** (*ittifāq*) and **confusions** (*ishtibāh*), as with names; and affiliations sometimes take place as nicknames
- and the reasons for these [because it may be contrary to the obvious].
- The *mawālī*: topwise [patrons and masters], and bottomwise [clients and freedmen],
- male and female siblings,
- and the etiquette of the shaykh and the student.
- It includes the age of procurement and conveyance; the manner of writing ḥadīth, reading [the shaykh's own narrations] back to the shaykh, audition, recital, and traveling for ḥadīth;
- One should also how ḥadīth is compiled: according to chains of narrators (*masānīd*), subject matter (*abwāb*), defects (*'ilal*), or keywords (*aṭrāf*); and knowing the historical context for the ḥadīth. One of the shaykhs of al-Qaḍi Abū Ya'lā bin al-Farrā' wrote about it.

They have written books in most of these genres. This is a basic list mentioning definitions without examples. It is difficult to be thorough, so consult the longer books.

Allah is the One Who grants success. He is the Guider. There is no god except He.

والمُفْرَدَةِ،

والْكُنَى، وَالأَلْقَابِ،

والأَنْسَابِ، وَتَقَعُ إِلَى القَبَائِلِ وَالأَوْطَانِ: بِلاداً، أَوْ ضِيَاعاً، أَوْ سِكَكاً، أَوْ مُجَاوَرَةً، وَإِلَى الصَّنَائِعِ وَالحِرَفِ: وَيَقَعُ فِيهَا الاتِّفَاقُ وَالاشْتِبَاهُ كَالأَسْمَاءِ، وَقَدْ تَقَعُ أَلْقَاباً. وَمَعْرِفَةُ أَسْبَابِ ذَلِكَ، وَمعرفةِ المَوَالِي مِنْ أَعْلَى وَمِنْ أَسْفَلَ: بالرِّقِّ، أَوْ بالحِلْفِ، وَمَعْرِفَةُ الإِخْوَةِ وَالأَخَوَاتِ.

وَمَعْرِفَةُ آدَابِ الشَّيْخِ وَالطَّالِبِ، وَسِنِّ التَّحَمُّلِ وَالأَدَاءِ، وَصِفَةِ كِتَابَةِ الحَدِيثِ وَعَرْضِهِ، وَسَمَاعِهِ، وَإِسْمَاعِهِ، وَالرِّحْلَةِ فِيهِ، وَتَصْنِيفِهِ: إِمَّا عَلَى المَسَانِيدِ، أَوِ الأَبْوَابِ، أَوِ العِلَلِ، أَوِ الأَطْرَافِ.

ومعرفة سَبَبِ الحَدِيثِ: وَقَدْ صَنَّفَ فِيهِ بَعْضُ شُيُوخِ القَاضِي أَبي يَعْلَى بن الفَرَّاءِ.

وَصَنَّفُوا فِي غَالِبِ هذِهِ الأَنْوَاعِ. وَهِيَ نَقْلٌ مَحْضٌ، ظَاهِرَةُ التَّعْرِيفِ، مُسْتَغْنِيَةٌ عَنِ التَّمْثِيلِ، وَحَصْرُها مُتَعَسِّرٌ: فَلْتُرَاجَعْ لَهَا مَبْسُوطَاتُهَا.

والله المُوَفِّقُ وَالهَادِي، لا إله إلاَّ هُوَ.

التذكرة

The Memorandum

by

IBN MULAQQIN

AL-TADHKIRAH

In the name of Allah Most Merciful and Beneficent.

1 *Introduction*

I praise Allah for His bounties. I thank him for His signs. I supplicate upon the most noble of creation Muḥammad, and upon his household, and give salutations.

To commence: I have taken these memorandums in ḥadīth sciences through which novices become acquainted and experts become clear-sighted from my book *Al-Muqniʿ*. I seek Allah through its being beneficial, since this is in His hand and His ability.

2 *Categories of Ḥadīths*

There are three categories of ḥadīths: **sound** (*ṣaḥīḥ*), **fair** (*ḥasan*), and **weak** (*ḍaʿīf*).

Sound is what is free of **aspersion** (*ṭaʿn*) in its ascription (*isnād*) and **content** (*matn*). It includes those that are "agreed upon," which are those which the Two Sheikhs [al-Bukhārī and Muslim] placed in their two Ṣaḥīḥs [*Ṣaḥīḥ al-Bukhārī*, and *Ṣaḥīḥ Muslim*].

Fair (*ḥasan*) is that which has an ascription [whose members are] lesser in memory and precision than the first category [i.e., sound].

التذكرة

بسم الله الرحمن الرحيم

١ مقدمة

الله أحمد على نعمائه، وأشكره على آلائه، وأصلي على أشرف الخلق محمد وآله، وأسلم.

وبعد: فهذه تذكرة في علوم الحديث، يتنبه بها المبتدي، ويتبصر بها المنتهي، اقتضبتها من «المقنع» تأليفي. وإلى الله أرغب في النفع بها، إنه بيده، والقادر عليه.

٢ أقسام الحديث

أقسام الحديث ثلاثة: صحيح، وحسن، وضعيف.

فالصحيح: ما سلم من الطعن في إسناده ومتنه. ومنه المتفق عليه، وهو ما أودعه الشيخان في «صحيحيهما».

والحسن: ما كان إسناده دون الأول في الحفظ والإتقان.

The phrase "**strong report**" (*al-qawiy*) includes fair and sound reports.

Weak (*ḍaʿīf*) is neither of the above.

3 *Types of Report-related Knowledge*

There are over eighty topics related to ḥadīths.

1. A **grounded report** (*musnad*) is a report whose chain is connected to the Prophet ﷺ. It is also called **connected** (*mawṣūl*)

2. A **continuous report** (*muttaṣal*) is that which has a continuous chain, whether it is **raised** or arrested. It is also called **connected** (*mawṣūl*).

3. A **raised-chain (Prophetic) report** (*marfūʿ*) is one attributed to the Prophet ﷺ (specifically), whether it is continuous or otherwise.

4. A **halted-chain (Companion) report** (*mawqūf*) is a statement, action, or the like, narrated from a Companion, whether continuous or severed. It is qualified when used with others [non-Companions], like "So-and-so halted it at ʿAṭāʾ" for example, and the like.

5. A **severed-chain (sub-Companion) report** (*maqṭūʿ*) is a statement or action ending at a Successor [the generation below the Companions] (*tābiʿ*).

6. A **broken-chained** (*munqataʿ*) report is one whose chain is not connected, regardless of how.

7. An **expedient report** (*mursal*) is a Successor – even one who is not major – saying "The Messenger of Allah ﷺ said…"

ويعمّه والذي قبله اسم الخبر القوي.

والضعيف: ما ليس واحدا منهما.

٣ أنواع علم الحديث

وأنواعه زائدة على الثمانين:

١ . المسند: وهو ما اتصل إسناده إلى النبي ﷺ. ويسمى موصولا أيضا.

٢ . والمتصل: وهو ما اتصل إسناده مرفوعا كان أو موقوفا، ويسمى موصولا أيضا.

٣. والمرفوع: وهو ما أضيف إلى النبي (خاصة)، متصلا كان أو غيره.

٤ . والموقوف: وهو المروي عن الصحابة قولا أو فعلا أو نحوه، متصلا كان أو منقطعا. ويستعمل في غيرهم مقيدا، فيقال: «وقفه فلان على عطاء مثلا، ونحوه»

٥ . والمقطوع: وهو الموقوف على التابعي قولا أو فعلا.

٦ . والمنقطع: وهو ما لم يتصل إسناده من أي وجه كان.

٧. والمرسل: وهو قول التابعي – وإن لم يكن كبيرا –: «قال رسول الله ﷺ ... ».

8. These reports include those with **hidden expedience** (*irsāl khafī*).

9. The **problematic report** (*muʿaḍal*) is when a **lacuna** [*saqṭ*] consists in two or more [consecutive] narrators. It is also called a **broken-chained report** (*munqaṭiʿ*). Every problematic report is broken-chained, but not the opposite.

10. The **suspended** (*muʿallaq*) report is when one or more [narrators] are removed from the beginning of its chain.

11. The **indecisive-transmission terminology report** (*muʿanʿan*) is that which comes including the phrase "from (*ʿan*)", like "So-and-so from so-and-so." It is a **continuous report** (*mutaṣṣal*) if it is not to camouflage (*tadlīs*) and their meeting is possible.

13. Camouflaging (*tadlīs*) is offensive since it suggests they met and were contemporaries. It is done by someone saying, "So-and-so says...." From sheikhs it is more subtle.

13. The **anomalous report** (*shādhdh*) is what a trustworthy narrator narrates contrary to what more trustworthy narrators narrate.

14. The **disclaimed report** (*munkar*) is a report that comes only from an individual who is neither skillful nor well-known for memorization.

15. The **unique report** (*fard*) is one that is unique amongst all narrators [**absolutely-unique report** (*fard muṭlaq*)] or a specific aspect [**relatively-unique report** (*fard nisbī*)], like unique to Meccans, and the like.

16. The **uncommon report** (*gharīb*) is when the uniqueness occurs with someone like al-Zuhrī whose ḥadīths are collected.

٨. ومنه ما خفي إرساله.

٩. والمعضل: وهو ما سقط من إسناده اثنان فأكثر. ويسمى منقطعا أيضا. فكل معضل منقطع، ولا عكس.

١٠. والمعلق: هو ما حذف من مبتدإ إسناده واحد فأكثر.

١١. والمعنعن: وهو ما أتي فيه بلفظة «عن»، كـ «فلان عن فلان»، وهو متصل إن لم يكن تدليسا، وأمكن اللقاء.

١٢. والتدليس: وهو مكروه لأنه يوهم اللقاء والمعاصرة، بقوله: «قال فلان ...» وهو في الشيوخ أخف.

١٣. والشاذ: وهو ما روى الثقة مخالفا لرواية الثقات.

١٤. والمنكر: وهو ما تفرد به واحد غير متقن ولا مشهور بالحفظ.

١٥. والفرد: وهو ما تفرد به واحد عن جميع الرواة، أو جهة خاصة، كقولهم: «تفرد به أهل مكة»، ونحوه.

١٦. والغريب: وهو ما تفرد به واحد عن الزهري وشبهه ممن يجمع حديثه.

17. If only two or three narrated it, it is called the **rare report** (*ʿazīz*).

18. If a group narrates it, it is called the **well-known report** (*mashhūr*).

19. It includes the **mass-transmitted report** (*mutawātir*): a group report which in itself coveys knowledge of its being true.

20. The **well-circulated report** (*mustafīḍ*) is that which has more than three narrators at every level [of its chain].

21. The **defective report** (*muʿallal*) is one in which a defect (*ʿillah*) harmful to its soundness has been observed, even though it appears to be free of it.

22. The **inconsistent report** (*muḍṭarib*) is that which is narrated in various ways that are equal [without preponderance of one ascription over the other].

23. An **interpolated report** (*mudraj*) is one in which an addition has occurred in its content [**content-interpolated** (*mudraj al-matn*)] or the like [e.g., **chain-interpolated** (*mudraj al-sanad*)].

24. The **forged report** (*mawḍūʿ*) is contrived and created. It can also be nicknamed **rejected** (*mardūd*), **discarded** (*matrūk*), **void** (*bāṭil*), and **spoiled** (*mufsad*).

25. The **topsy-turvy report** (*maqlūb*) is ascribing a ḥadīth to someone other than its narrators.

26. **Elevated** (*ʿālī*) is a merit which is sought after. It occurs when there is closeness to the Prophet ﷺ or one of the imāms of ḥadīth, through prior death of the narrator, and audition.

27. **Descended** (*nāzil*) is the opposite of elevated.

١٧. فإن انفرد اثنان أو ثلاثة، سمي عزيزا.

١٨. فإن رواه جماعة سمي مشهورا.

١٩. ومنه المتواتر: وهو خبر جماعة يفيد بنفسه العلم بصدقه.

٢٠. والمستفيض: وهو ما زاد رواته في كل مرتبة على ثلاثة.

٢١. والمعلل: وهو ما اطلع فيه على علة قادحة في صحته، مع السلامة عنها ظاهرا.

٢٢. والمضطرب: وهو ما يروى على أوجه مختلفة متساوية.

٢٣. والمدرج: وهو زيادة تقع في المتن ونحوه.

٢٤. والموضوع: وهو المختلق المصنوع. وقد يلقب بـ «المردود»، و«المتروك»، و«الباطل»، و«المفسد».

٢٥. والمقلوب: وهو إسناد الحديث إلى غير راويه.

٢٦. والعالي: وهو فضيلة مرغوب فيها، ويحصل بالقرب من النبي ومن أحد الأئمة في الحديث، وبتقدم وفاة الراوي، والسماع.

٢٧. والنازل: وهو ضد العالي.

28. **Reconciliation** (*mukhtalif*) is when two ḥadīths appear to disagree and they are reconciled, or one of them is judged preponderant over the other.

29. A **dot-distorted report** (*muṣaḥḥaf*) is when the pronunciation and meaning are changed [due to dots, e.g., ـبـتـثـنـيـ. **Vowel-distorted** (*muḥarraf*) is due to vowels, e.g., ـبُـبِـبَـ].

30. **Pattern-chain narration** (*musalsal*) is when the narrators of the chain narrate it while affecting a specific quality or manner. It being done with sound reports is rare.

31. **Evaluation** (*iʿtibār*) is, for example, Ḥamād bin Salamah narrates a ḥadīth without a corroborating chain from Ayyūb from Ibn Sirīn from Abū Hurayrah.

32. **Corroboration** (*mutābah*) is someone other than Ḥammād narrated from Ayyūb. This is **complete corroboration** (*mutābaʿ tāmmah*).

33. A **witness-report** (*shāhid*) is when a ḥadīth [with similar content] is narrated with [its content conveying] the same meaning.

34. **Additions from trustworthy narrators** are accepted, according to the masses.

35. An **addition in continuous attribution** is when one or more people are mistakenly added to the chain.

36. The attributes of the narrator include being upright (*ʿadl*) and accurate (*ḍabṭ*). [Knowing their attributes] includes knowing [causes for] **discreditation** (*jarḥ*) and **commendation** (*taʿdīl*), clarifying the age of procurement (which is at discernment, typically at 5 years), and the manner of audition and conveyance.

٢٨. والمختلف: وهو أن يأتي حديثان متعارضان في المعنى ظاهرا، فيوفق بينهما، أو يرجّح أحدهما على الآخر.

٢٩. والمصحَّف: وهو تغيير لفظ أو معنى. وتارة يقع في المتن، وتارة في الإسناد. وفيه تصانيف.

٣٠. والمسلسل: وهو ما تتابع رجال إسناده على صفة أو حالة. وقل فيه الصحيح.

٣١. والاعتبار: وهو أن يروي حماد بن سلمة -مثلا- حديثا، لا يتابع عليه، عن أيوب، عن ابن سيرين، عن أبي هريرة..

٣٢. والمتابعة: أن يرويه عن أيوب غير حماد. وهي المتابعة التامة.

٣٣. والشاهد: أن يروى حديث آخر بمعناه.

٣٤. وزيادة الثقات. والجمهور على قبولها.

٣٥. والمزيد في متصل الأسانيد: وهو أن يزاد في الإسناد رجل فأكثر غلطا.

٣٦. وصفة الراوي: وهو العدل الضابط. ويدخل فيه معرفة الجرح والتعديل، وبيان سن السماع -وهو التمييز- ويحصل له في خمس غالبا، وكيفية السماع والتحمل.

37. Writing ḥadīth is permissible according to consensus. It turns aspirations towards its accuracy.

38. The paths of narration are eight: hearing the sheikh's utterance [of the narration]; reading it to the sheikh; the various forms of **authorization** (*ijāzah*); it being put into one's hands (*munāwalah*); the sheikh writing it to him (*mukātabah*); announcement; via bequest (*waṣiyyah*); and (finding it written (*wijādah*).

39. The description of the narration and its conveyance, which includes narrating by paraphrasing the meaning, and abridging the hadith.

40. The etiquette of those who narrate ḥadīths and those who seek them.

41. Knowing its strange vocabulary and dialects, explaining its meanings, and deriving its legal rulings;

42. attributing it to the Companion, Follower, and their followers.

43. In doing this, one needs to know the five [legal] rulings, which are: obligation (*wujūb*), recommendation (*nadb*), prohibition (*taḥrīm*), blameworthiness (*karāhah*), and permissiveness (*ibāḥah*).

And to know their attachments, which include:

(1) **Particular** (*khāṣṣ*). It is what indicates a single meaning.

(2) **General** (*ʿāmm*). It is what indicates two things from a single aspect.

(3) **Absolute** (*muṭlaq*). It is what indicates a single meaning without an identifier or it being contingent.

٣٧. وكتابة الحديث: وهو جائز إجماعا. وتصرف الهمة إلى ضبطه.

٣٨. وأقسام طرق الرواية: وهي ثمانية: السماع من لفظ الشيخ، والقراءة عليه، والإجازة بأنواعها، والمناولة، والمكاتبة، والإعلام، والوصية، والوجادة.

٣٩. وصفة الرواية وأدائها. ويدخل فيه الرواية بالمعنى، واختصار الحديث.

٤٠. وآداب المحدث وطالب الحديث.

٤١. ومعرفة غريبه ولغته، وتفسير معانيه، واستنباط أحكامه.

٤٢. وعزوه إلى الصحابة والتابعين وأتباعهم.

٤٣. ويحتاج في ذلك إلى معرفة الأحكام الخمسة، وهي: الوجوب، والندب، والتحريم، والكراهة، والإباحة.

ومتعلقاتها من:

الخاص: وهو ما دلَّ على معنى واحد.

والعام: وهو ما دل على شيئين من جهة واحدة.

والمطلق: وهو ما دل على معنى واحد مع عدم تعيين في ولا شرط.

(4) **Qualified** (*muqayyad*). It is what indicates one meaning that is contingent upon something else.

(5) **Detailed** (*mufaṣṣal*). It is that whose intended meaning is known from its wording without requiring something else for its clarification.

(6) **Explained** (*mufassar*). It is that whose intended meaning is not clear and requires something else for its clarification.

44. Determining preponderance between narrations is done via the quantity of narrators when there is equality in the memorization, via the quantity when they are distinct, and other ways.

45. Knowing **abrogating** (*nāsikh*) and **abrogated** (*mansūkh*).

46. Knowing the Companions (may Allah be pleased with them),

47. their Successors (may Allah have mercy upon them);

48. **seniors-from-juniors narrations** (*akābir ʿan ṣaghāʾir*) (like the Prophet ﷺ narrating from Tamīm al-Dārī, [Abū Bakr al-Ṣiddīq,] and others);

49. peers narrating from peers [**peer narration** (*aqrān*)] (like al-Thawrī and Abū Ḥanīfah from Mālik: "Young girls are more rightful to themselves than their guardians.");

50. **fathers-from-sons narration** (*al-ābā ʿand al-abnāʾ*), (like al-ʿAbbās narrating from his son al-Faḍal – and the opposite), and likewise mothers narrating from their sons.

والمقيد: وهو ما دل على معنى مع اشتراط آخر.

والمفصل: وهو ما عرف المراد من لفظه، ولم يفتقر في البيان إلى غيره.

والمفسر: وهو ما لا يفهم المراد منه، ويفتقر إلى غيره.

٤٤. والتراجيح بين الرواة من جهة كثرة العدد مع الاستواء في الحفظ، من جهة العدد أيضا، مع التباين فيه . وغير ذلك.

٤٥. ومعرفة ناسخه ومنسوخه.

٤٦. ومعرفة الصحابة.

٤٧. وأتباعهم.

٤٨. ومن روى من الأكابر عن الأصاغر؛ كرواية النبي ﷺ عن تميم الداريوالصِّدِّيق، وغيرهما.

ويلقب أيضا برواية الفاضل عن المفضول، ورواية الشيخ عن التلميذ؛ كرواية الزهري، ويحيى بن سعيد، وربيعة، وغيرهم، عن مالك.

٤٩. ورواية النظير عن النظير؛ كالثوري وأبي حنيفة عن مالك حديث: «الأيم أحق بنفسها من وليها».

٥٠. ومعرفة رواية الآباء عن الأبناء: كرواية العباس عن ابنه الفضل، وعكسه. وكذا رواية الأم عن ولدها.

51. Knowing **reciprocal narration** (*mudabbaj*). It is when peers narrate from one another. It is not reciprocal narration when one narrates from another and the other does not narrate from him.

52. Knowing: **narration of brothers and sisters**, like ʿUmar and Zayd – both sons of al-Khaṭṭāb [i.e., ʿUmar bin al-Khaṭṭab and Zayd bin al-Khaṭṭāb];

53. those who have been narrated from by two individuals who died many years apart, like al-Sirāj: al-Bukhāri narrated from him as did al-Khaffāf, and there are at least 137 years between their deaths;

54. Companions who have only a single narrator, like Muḥammad ibn Ṣafwān whose only narrator is al-Shaʿbī;

55. those who were known by numerous names or titles, like [the exegete] Muḥammad bin al-Sā'ib al-Kalbī al-mufassir.

56. Knowing names, agnomens, and nicknames.

57. Knowing those individuals [of the above], and who is well-known by their name but not their agnomen, and the opposite;

58. those whose names match their father's name.

59. [names which match in writing but differ in pronunciation] **homographic-heterophonic** (*mu'talif wa-mukhtalif*);

٥١. ومعرفة المُدَبَّجِ: وهو رواية الأقران بعضهم عن بعض. فإن روى أحدهما عن الآخر، ولم يرو الآخر عنه، فغير مدبج.

٥٢. ومعرفة رواية الإخوة والأخوات، كعمر وزيد ابني الخطاب.

٥٣. ومن اشترك عنه الرواية اثنان تباعد ما بين وفاتيهما؛ كالسراج، فإن البخاري روى عنه، وكذا الخفّاف، وبين وفاتيهما مائة وسبع وثلاثون أو أكثر.

٥٤. ومن لم يرو عنه إلا واحد من الصحابة فمن بعدهم؛ كمحمد بن صفوان، لم يروِ عنه غير الشعبي.

٥٥. ومن عُرف بأسماء أو نعوت متعددة؛ كمحمد بن السائب الكلبي المفسر.

٥٦. ومعرفة الأسماء والكنى والألقاب.

٥٧. ومعرفة مفردات ذلك، ومن اشتهر بالاسم دون الكنية، وعكسه.

٥٨. ومن وافق اسمه اسم أبيه.

٥٩. والمؤتلف والمختلف.

60. [the names of narrators and the names of their fathers and forefathers match though they are different individuals] **same-name different-identity narrator** (*mutaffiq wa-muftariq*);

61. combinations of the above two;

62. [when names match but differ in their fathers, or the opposite] **same-name different-father-or-son narrators** (*mutashābih*);

63. those ascribed to someone other than their father (like Bilāl bin Ḥimāmah);

64. those affiliated to something where what is intended differs from what immediately comes to mind (like Abū Masʿūd al-Badrī: he resided there [at Badr] but did not participate [in its battle]);

65. **anonymous mentions** (*mubhamāt*);

66. dates of birth and death.

67. Knowing trustworthy and weak [narrators] (and for those about whom there is disagreement, refer to [Imām al-Dhahabī's] *Mīzān al-iʿtidāl*);

68. trustworthy narrators whose narrations became jumbled at the end of their lives – their narrations are accepted before this, but not after;

69. those whose books burned or were lost, and subsequently returned to their memory and did poorly.

70. Those who narrated and forgot, and then narrated from someone who had narrated from him.

٦٠. والمتفق والمفترق.

٦١. وما تركب منهما.

٦٢. والمتشابه.

٦٣. والمنسوب إلى غير أبيه: كبلال بن حِمامَةَ.

٦٤. والنسبة التي يسبق إلى الفهم منها شيء، وهي بخلافه؛ كأبي مسعود البدري، فإنه نزلها، ولم يشهدها.

٦٥. والمبهمات.

٦٦. والتواريخ والوفيات.

٦٧. ومعرفة الثقات والضعفاء؛ ومن اختلف فيه، فيرجح بـ «الميزان».

٦٨. ومن اختلط في آخر عمره من الثقات، وخَرِف منهم. فمن روى قَبْلَ ذلك عنهم قُبل، وإلا فلا.

٦٩. ومن احترقت كتبه أو ذهبت، فيرجع إلى حفظه فساء.

٧٠. ومن حدث ونسي، ثم روى عمن روى عنه.

71. Knowing the **synchronous layers** (*ṭabaqāt*) of narrators and scholars;

72. the *mawāli* [whether patrons and masters, or clients and freedmen],

73. tribes, lands, crafts and professions, and their traits.

4 *Closing*

This is the end of the memorandum. It is a quick boost for novices and an introduction to the book previously mentioned at the beginning [*Al-Muqniʿ*], as it gathers the useful lessons and peculiarities, its most interesting points, and its precious gems.

I finished preparing these notes in approximately two hours, on Friday morning, 27 Jumādah al-Awwal 763AH. May Allah make part of it excellent and may the rest be in goodness. Amin.

٧١. ومعرفة طبقات الرواة والعلماء.

٧٢. والموالي.

٧٣. والقبائل، والبلاد، والصناعة، والحلي.

٤ آخر «التذكرة»

وهي عُجالة للمبتدي فيه، ومدخل للتأليف السالف المشار إليه أولا، فإنه جامع لفوائد هذا العلم وشوارده، ومهماته، وفرائِده. ولله الحمد على تيسيره وأمثاله.

قال مؤلفه رحمه الله: فرغتُ من تحرير هذه «التذكرة» في نحو ساعتين، من صبيحة يوم الجمعة، سابع عشرين جماد الأولى، عام ثلاث وستين وسبع مائة، أحسن الله بعضها، وما بعدها في خير، آمين.

INDEX

To facilitate finding terms, Arabic entries begin with a lowercase letter and English with an uppercase letter. Arabic entries come together before English. The word order ignores dots, macrons, and the ʿayn, so Ḍ is with D, and Ā and ʿA with A.

al-ābā ʿan al-abnāʾ 20, 46
ʿadl 6, 42
afʿal 26
āhād 4, 6
akābir ʿan ṣaghāʾir 20, 46
akdhab al-nās 26
akhbaranī 22
ʿālī 40
ʿāmm 44
ʿan 10, 22, 38
ʿan abīhi ʿan jaddihi 20
anbaʾanī 22
ʿanʿana 24
aqrān 20, 46
arjaḥ 6
āthār 18
aṭrāf 30
awthaq al-nās 26
ʿazīz 4, 40

Al-ʿAbbās 46
Abrogation 8, 46
Abū Bakr al-Ṣiddīq 46
Abū Ḥanīfah 46
Abū Hurayrah 42
Abū Masʿūd al-Badrī 50
Additions 42
Affiliation 24
Agnomen 28, 30, 48
Anonymous mentions 14, 50
Ascription 18
Aspersion 8, 12
ʿAṭāʾ 36
Attachment
  absolute 44
  detailed 46
  explained 46
  general 44
  particular 44
  qualified 46
Audition 42
Authorization 22, 24, 44
Ayyūb 42

badal 20
bāṭil 40

Bilāl bin Ḥimāmah 50
Al-Bukhārī 6, 34, 48

Chain 4, 10
  concurrent 18
  convergent 20
  descended 40
  elevated 40
Clarifier 14
Commendation 14, 26, 28, 42
Companion
  definition of 18
Compilation, manners of 30
Composite grading 6
Content 14
Contradiction or objection 8
Conveyance
  forms of 22
  manner of 42
  manners of 44
Corroboration 42
  complete 42
Criteria 6

ḍabṭ 42
ḍaʿīf 8
dajjāl 26
ḍaʿīf 34, 36

Decisive 8
Descent 20
Al-Dhahabī 50
Discreditation 26, 28, 42
  categories of 26

Elevation 20
  absolute 18
  relative 18

Evaluation 8, 42

fard 4, 38
  muṭlaq 4, 38
  nisbī 4, 8, 38
fāsiq 12
fīhi maqāl 26

Al-Faḍal 46
Al-Farrā', al-Qaḍi Abū Yaʿlā bin 30

ghaflah 12
gharābah 4
gharīb 4, 38

ḥaddathanī 22
ḥasan 34
  lā li-dhātihi bal bil-majmūʿ 16
  li-dhātih 6
  ṣaḥīḥ 6

Ḥadith
  ruling of writing 44
Ḥammād bin Salamah 42
Handshaking 20
Historical context 30
Homographic-heterophonic 24, 48

ibāḥah 44
ijāzah 22, 24, 44
ʿilal 30
iʿlām 24
ʿillah 40
ʿilm
  naẓarī 4
  yaqīnī 4
irsāl khafī 38

ishtibāh 30
isnād 18, 34
ittifāq 30
iʿtibār 8, 42

Ibn Sirīn 42
Innovation 16

jahālah 12, 14, 26
jamʿ 8
jarḥ 26, 28, 42

Al-Jūzajānī 16

kadhdhāb 26
karāhah 44
kataba ilayya 22
khabar 2
khāṣṣ 44
kunā 28
kunya 28

Al-Khaffāf 48
Knowledge 4, 40

layyin 26

Lacuna 8, 10, 38
Legal rulings 44

maḥfūẓ 6
majhūl
  al-ḥāl 14
  al-ʿayn 14
man ḥaddatha wa-nasiya 22
mansūkh 8, 46
maqbūl 8
maqlūb 12, 40
maqṭūʿ 18, 36
mardūd 40
marfūʿ 12, 18, 36
masānīd 30
mashhūr 4, 40
mastūr 14, 16
matn 8, 14, 34
matrūk 12, 40
mawālī 30, 52
mawḍūʿ 12, 40
mawqūf 12, 18, 36
mawṣūl 36
mazīd fī muttaṣil al-masānīd 12
maʿrūf 8
mubham 14
mubhamāt 14, 50
mudabbaj 20, 48
mudallas 10
mudallis 16, 24
al-mūḍiḥ 14
mudraj 40
  al-isnād 12
  al-matn 12, 40
  al-sanad 40
muḍṭarib 14, 40
mufaṣṣal 46
mufassar 46
mufradah 30
mufsad 40
muḥarraf 14, 42
muḥkam 8
mukātabah 24, 44
mukhālafah 12
mukhtalaṭ 16
mukhtalif 42
  al-ḥadīth 8
mukhtār 24
munāwalah 24, 44
munkar 8, 12, 38
munqaṭiʿ 10, 36, 38

muqayyad 46
mursal 10, 36
  khafī 10
mursil 16
muṣāfaḥah 20
muṣaḥāfah 24
muṣaḥḥaf 14, 42
musalsal 22, 42
musāwāt 20
musnad 18, 36
mustafīḍ 4, 40
mutābiᶜ 8, 42
  tāmmah 42
mutaffiq wa-muftariq 50
mu'talif wa-mukhtalif 24
mutashābih 24, 50
mutawātir 4, 40
muṭlaq 44
muttafiq wa-muftariq 24
muttaṣal 36, 38
muwāfaqa 18
muʾtalif wa-mukhtalif 48
muᶜallal 6, 12, 40
muᶜallaq 10, 38
muᶜanᶜan 38
muᶜāraḍah 8
muᶜḍal 10, 38

Mālik 46
Mīzān al-iᶜtidāl 50
Muḥammad bin al-Sāʾib al-Kalbī al-mufassir 48
Muḥammad ibn Ṣafwā 48
Mūsā ibn Ṭalḥa 10
Muslim 34

nadb 44
nāsikh 8, 46
nāwalanī 22
nāzil 40
nisbah 24
nuzūl 20

Narration
  fathers-from-sons 20, 46
  of brothers and sisters 48
  paths of 44
  pattern-chain 42
  peer 20, 46
  predecessor-successor 20
  reciprocal 20, 48
  seniors-from-juniors 20
  son-from-father or grandfather 20
Narrators
  anonymous 14
  attributes of 42
  contradicting others 12
  names exclusive to one person 30
  same-name different-father-or-son 24, 50
  same-name different-identity 24, 50
  single-report 14
  synchronous layers of 26, 52
  those-who-narrated-and-forgot 22
  unknown 14, 26
Al-Nasā'ī 16

parity 20

qāla 10
qarāʾin 12
qaraʾtu ᶜalayhi 22
al-qawī 36
quriʾa ᶜalayhi wa-ana asmaᶜu

22

Reporter
  camouflaging 24
  expedient 16
  of unknown status 14
  unidentifiable 14
  veiled 14, 16
Reports
  determining preponderance between 46
  reconcilable 8
  reconciliation 8, 42
Reports, types of 2
  abrogated 8, 46
  abrogating 8, 46
  absolutely-unique 4, 38
  accepted 8
  already-connected-chain 12
  anomalous 6, 16, 38
  bequeathed-book 24
  broken-chained 10, 36, 38
  camouflaged 10, 38
  chain-interpolated 12, 40
  connected 36
  content-interpolated 12, 40
  continuous 36
  continuous-chain 6, 38
  corroborative-chain 8
  defective 6, 12, 40
  discarded 12, 40
  disclaimed 8, 12, 38
  dot-distorted 14, 42
  expedient 10, 36
  fair 34
    in-itself 6
    on-the-whole 16
  fair-sound 6
  forged 12, 40
  found 24
  grounded 18, 36
  halted-chain (Companion) 12, 18, 36
  hidden-expedient 10, 38
  inconsistent 14, 40
  indecisive-transmission terminology 24, 38
  interpolated 40
  jumbled 16
  mass-transmitted 4, 40
  non-Prophetic 18
  positively established 8
  problematic 10, 38
  public announcement 24
  raised-chain (Prophetic) 18, 36
  rare 4, 40
  rejected 40
  relatively-unique 4, 8, 38
  severed-chain (sub-Companion) 18, 36
  solitary 4, 6
  sound 6, 34
    in-itself 6
  spoiled 40
  strong 36
  suspended 10, 38
  topsy-turvy 12, 40
  uncommon 4, 38
  unique 4, 38
  void 40
  vowel-distorted 14, 42
  weak 8, 34, 36
  well-circulated 4, 40
  well-known 4, 40
  well-preserved 6
  well-recognized 8
  witness 8, 42

sābiq wa-lāḥiq 20
ṣaḥīḥ 6, 34
bi-dhātihi 6
samiʿtu 22
sanad 4, 6, 10
saqṭ 8, 38
sayyiʾ al-ḥifẓ 26
shādhdh 6, 16, 38
shāfahanī 22
shāhid 8, 42
shaykh 26
shurūṭ 6

Al-Shaʿbī 48
Shuʿbah 18
Al-Sirāj 48
Successor
definition of 18

ṭabaqāt 26, 52
tābiʿ 36
tadlīs 38
taḥrīm 44
tāmm al-ḍabṭ 6
tarjīḥ 8
tawaqquf 8
tazkiya 28
taʿdīl 14, 26, 28, 42
ṭaʿn 8, 12, 34
thābit 8
thiqah ḥāfiẓ 26
thiqah thiqah 26

Tamīm al-Dārī 46
Al-Thawrī 46

ʿulūw 20
muṭlaq 18
nisbī 18

ʿUmar bin al-Khaṭṭab 48

waḍḍāʿ 26
wahm 12
waṣiyyah 44
bil-kitāb 24
wijādah 24, 44
al-wuḥdān 14
wujūb 44

Zayd bin al-Khaṭṭab 48
Al-Zuhrī 38

CPSIA information can be obtained
at www.ICGtesting.com
Printed in the USA
LVHW112133310519
619780LV00001B/5/P

9 780985 884062